FASHION DESIGN

COLORING BOOK FOR GIRLS

This book belong to:

Copyright © 2022.

All rights reserved.
No part of this book may be
reproduced in any form or
by any electronic or
mechanical means,
including information storage
and retrieval systems, without
written permission from
the author, except for
the use of brief quotations
in a book review.

Color Test Page

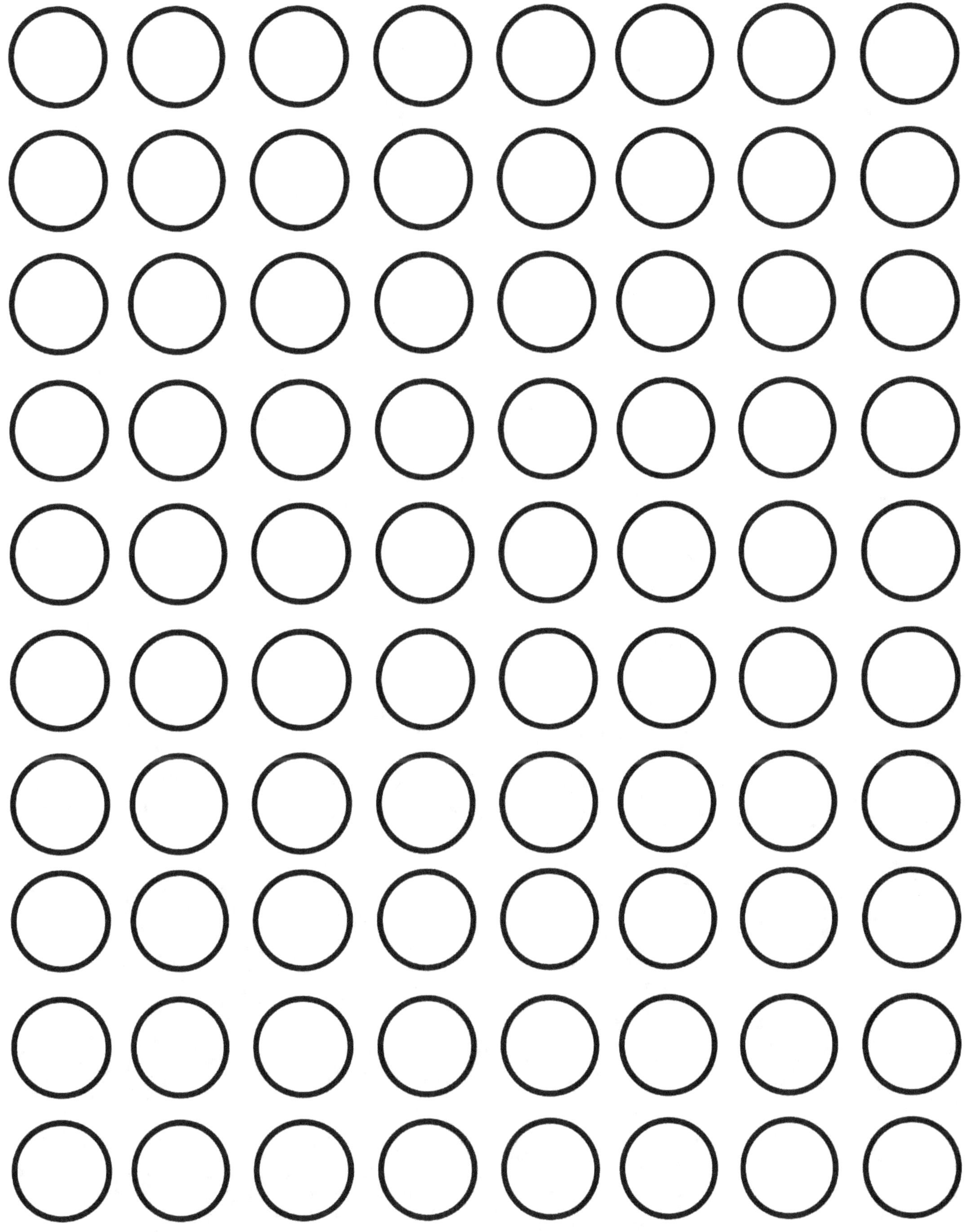

California
Follower

California

BETTER
THAN GOOD

can't buy
my love.

SHE CONQUERS ALL

FULL OF LOVE
NEW YORK
EST. 1986

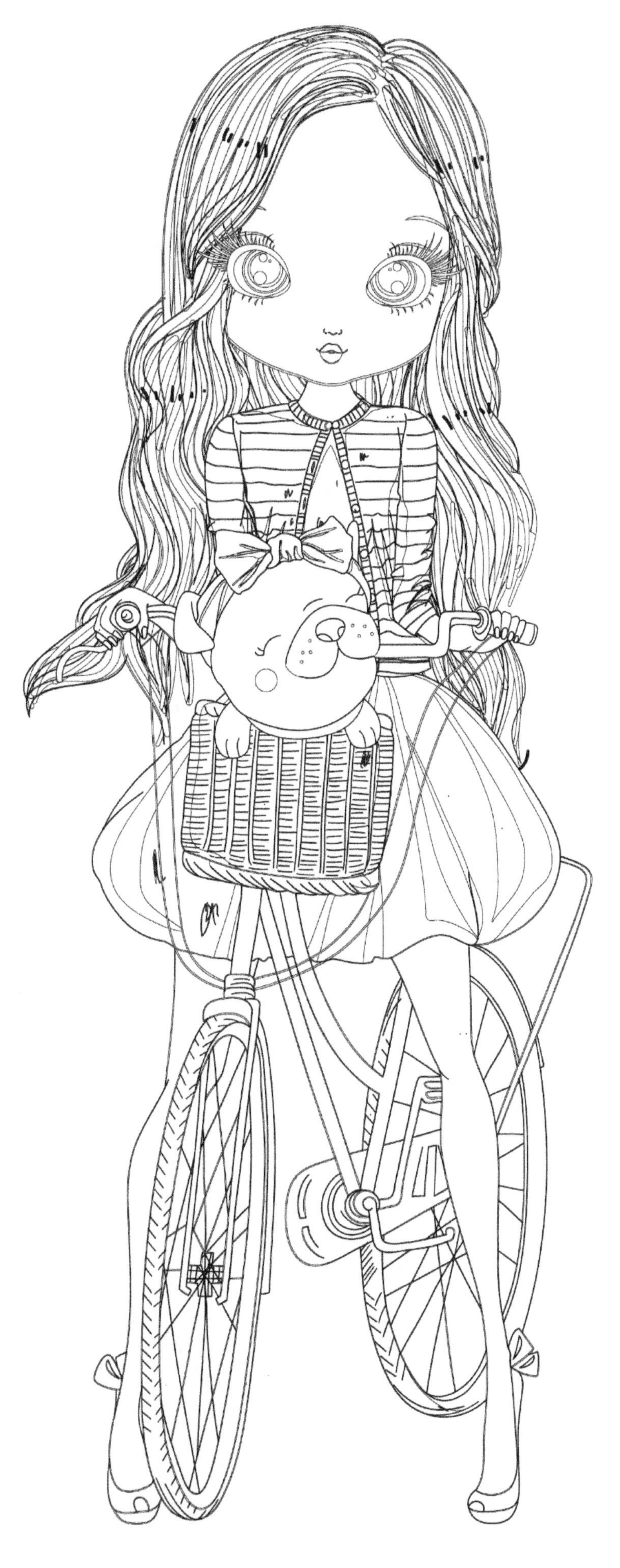

LOVE

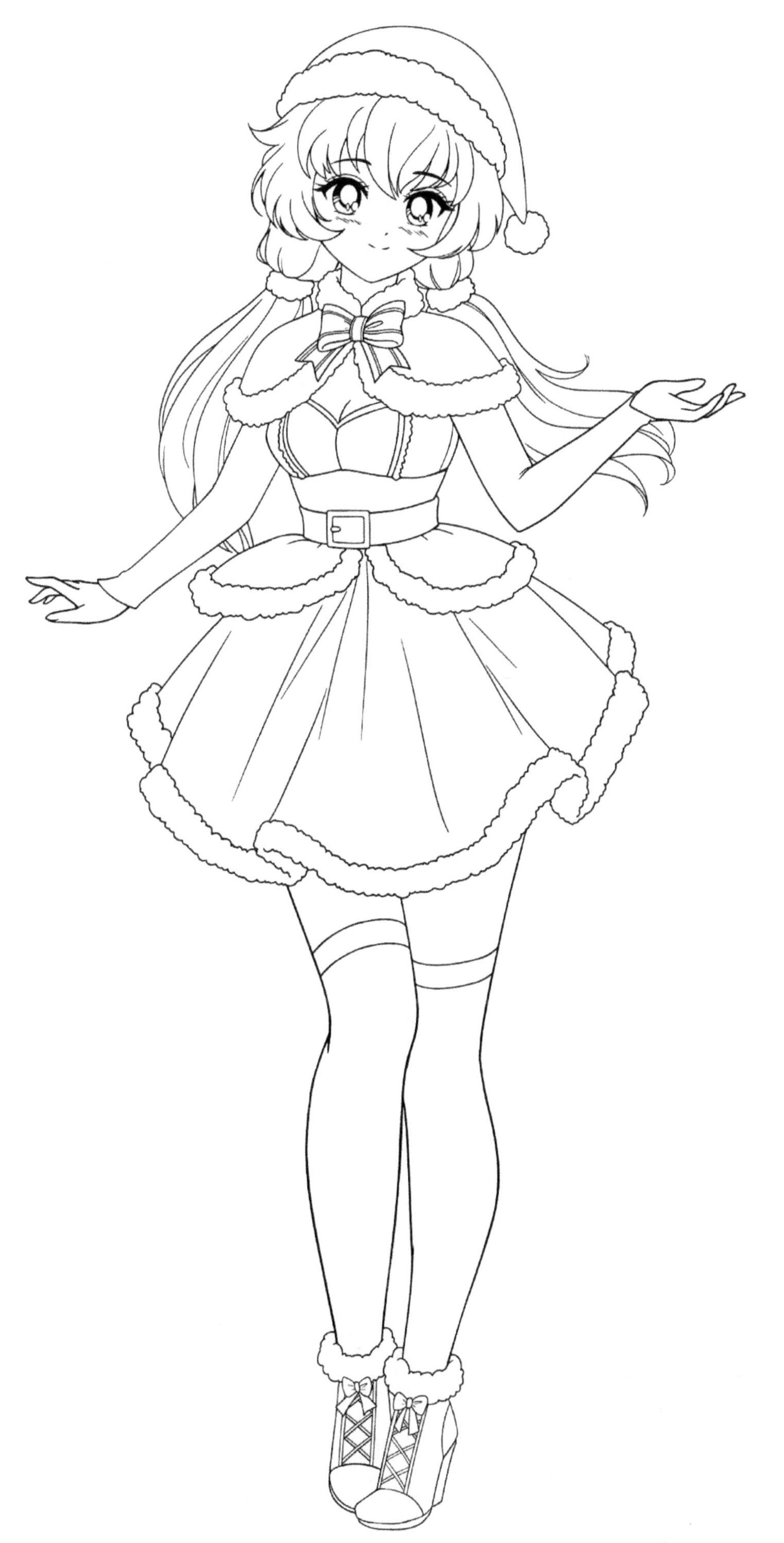

www.ingramcontent.com/pod-product-compliance
Lightning Source LLC
Chambersburg PA
CBHW081222260726

48653CB00010BB/3743